Original title:
Threads of Red

Copyright © 2024 Swan Charm
All rights reserved.

Author: Sebastian Sarapuu
ISBN HARDBACK: 978-9908-1-2668-5
ISBN PAPERBACK: 978-9908-1-2669-2
ISBN EBOOK: 978-9908-1-2670-8

The Ties that Bind

In whispers soft, we share our dreams,
A bond unseen, yet brightly gleams.
Through trials faced, we stand so tall,
Together we rise, together we fall.

Hands grasped tight, as storms may rage,
Every chapter, we turn the page.
With laughter light, and tears we share,
A tapestry woven, beyond compare.

In quiet nights, our hearts align,
Two souls entwined, a love divine.
With every challenge, we will find,
The strength in pain, the ties that bind.

As seasons change, and years go by,
We cherish moments, both low and high.
A journey marked, with joy and strife,
In every heartbeat, a shared life.

So here we stand, through thick and thin,
A testament true, to love within.
In every glance, and every sigh,
The ties that bind, will never die.

A Ruby Narrative

In twilight's glow, a ruby bright,
A story held, in crimson light.
Each facet gleams, with whispers old,
Of love and loss, in hues of gold.

Once it lay, in earth's embrace,
A treasure formed, in hidden place.
With every cut, the tale unfolds,
A journey told, in whispers bold.

Through battles fought, and passions shared,
The ruby's heart, both fierce and scared.
In lovers' hands, it sparkles clear,
A legacy forged, through joy and fear.

Within its glow, a world resides,
Of dreams and hopes, where time abides.
In every sheen, a promise made,
Of timeless love that will not fade.

So as you gaze, upon this stone,
Remember well, you are not alone.
For in this ruby, our hearts combine,
A narrative rich, forever divine.

Embered Traces

In the quiet glow of night,
Whispers of dreams take flight.
Fading sparks of what was bright,
Leaving shadows, soft and slight.

Memories linger, bittersweet,
Echoes of love in heartbeats.
Ashes fall like gentle rain,
Carrying both joy and pain.

Time moves on, but embers stay,
Guiding lost souls on their way.
In the darkness, we find light,
Tracing paths of hope in night.

With every breath, we rise anew,
Finding strength in what we rue.
Embered traces of the past,
A reminder that love can last.

Dancing flames in twilight's hold,
Stories of warmth in embers told.
Each flicker a chance to heal,
To reclaim the love we feel.

The Color of Heartache

On canvas stretched, emotions bleed,
A palette rich with pain and greed.
Hues of sorrow, shades of blue,
Capture all I lost in you.

The brush strokes tell a timeless tale,
Of laughter lost and hopes that pale.
Each tear a drop of crimson red,
Painting paths where dreams once fled.

Golden whispers start to fade,
In the shadows, love's charade.
Colorful scars that won't erase,
Marking every touched embrace.

Yet in the grey, a spark ignites,
Turning heartache into lights.
Artistry in all I feel,
The color of heartache, surreal.

A masterpiece forged in the pain,
Beauty rises from the rain.
With every stroke, the heart breaks free,
Finding solace in the sea.

Weaving Wounds and Wonders

Threads of sorrow intertwine,
In the fabric of design.
Stitching wounds with golden thread,
Creating warmth where love once bled.

Patterns formed from tears and laughter,
Every weave leads to hereafter.
Tapestries both bright and stark,
Charting journeys of the heart.

In the needle's gentle dance,
We find purpose, take a chance.
Wonders shimmer, wounds reveal,
A blend of pain that starts to heal.

Color bursts in every line,
Beneath the surface, hope will shine.
Fading echoes of what's been lost,
Rise anew, despite the cost.

Weaving dreams like threads in air,
Crafting love beyond despair.
Each knot an anchor, strong and true,
Binding wounds with wonders too.

Crimson Shadows Dance

Crimson shadows flicker low,
In the twilight's softened glow.
Ghostly figures move with grace,
Dancing through this haunted space.

Whispers of a bygone day,
Echo softly, drift away.
In the night, their secrets weave,
Tales of loss and love believe.

Moonlight bathes the ground in dreams,
Where silence sings and sorrow gleams.
Every step a memory traced,
In the shadows, time is faced.

Ebbing tides of heart's embrace,
Leave their mark, an airy lace.
Crimson threads of what we seek,
Binding moments, strong yet weak.

As the dance begins anew,
Life and death in shades of blue.
Crimson shadows, secrets tell,
In their depths, we find our spell.

Crimson Echoes

In shadows where whispers dwell,
Soft sighs of passion swell.
Crimson dreams in twilight's embrace,
Echoes linger, time can't erase.

A heart that beats, a silent plea,
Where hope blooms wild, and spirits free.
Lost in a dance, we twirl and spin,
The night is young, let love begin.

Beneath the stars, our stories blend,
In every curve, a journey penned.
Hands entwined, we chase the light,
Crimson echoes in the night.

Softest murmurs, secrets shared,
Within our souls, the cosmos bared.
Each heartbeat a vivid trace,
Of love's sweet song, a soft embrace.

When dawn arrives, we'll not forget,
The moments held, the paths we set.
In every hue, our memories glow,
Crimson echoes endlessly flow.

Stained with Emotion

Canvas of life, brushed in despair,
Colors collide, a heart laid bare.
Stains of joy and shadows of pain,
Each stroke a memory, love's sweet gain.

The brush moves slow, yet swift like time,
Crafting a tale in rhythm and rhyme.
Tears and laughter, textures unfold,
In vivid hues, our truth retold.

Layer by layer, the story builds,
With every tint, a dream fulfilled.
Passionate reds and calming blues,
In the masterpiece, we can't lose.

Palette of life, rich and profound,
In silence we feel, the beauty found.
Love's rich stain, a treasured token,
In this artwork, words unspoken.

When the final stroke has been laid,
We'll gaze upon what love has made.
Stained with emotion, we stand enthralled,
In colors of love, our souls are called.

The Weaver's Secret

Threads of gold in the moonlit night,
Twisting and turning, a dance of light.
The weaver spins with a gentle grace,
Crafting a tapestry time can't erase.

Each strand a memory, woven tight,
Stories entwined in the fabric's sight.
Laughter and sorrow, joy interlaced,
In every fiber, a truth embraced.

Patterns unfold with each passing day,
In the loom of fate, we find our way.
Colors of life, brilliant and bold,
In the weaver's hands, our futures unfold.

With nimble fingers, the secrets blend,
Past and present, through threads ascend.
The weaver knows what the heart seeks,
In quiet moments, the soul speaks.

As dawn breaks and shadows recede,
The weaver smiles, fulfilling a need.
In this creation, a tale so deep,
The weaver's secret, forever we keep.

Interlaced in Burgundy

Underneath the vine's embrace,
A dance of shadows, a secret place.
Burgundy whispers in delicate tones,
Where passions linger and sweetness hones.

In twilight's blush, our hands entwined,
A moment captured, forever aligned.
Promises bloom like roses in spring,
Interlaced hearts in the warmth we bring.

Beneath the boughs, time stands still,
Soft laughter echoes with gentle thrill.
In each other's gaze, the world fades away,
Interlaced in Burgundy, we choose to stay.

The night unfolds with a silken thread,
Stories whispered as we tread.
In every glance, a spark ignites,
Painting the dark with our shared lights.

As stars emerge in the velvet sky,
We weave our dreams and let them fly.
Interlaced in Burgundy, hearts run free,
In the vineyard's heart, it's you and me.

Hues of Heartstrings

In the glow of twilight hues,
Whispers dance on gentle breeze.
A symphony of vibrant muse,
Binding hearts with tender ease.

A canvas painted with pure light,
Colors blend in warm embrace.
Lost in dreams that take to flight,
Every shade reveals our grace.

Threads of gold in shadows weave,
Stories told in every glance.
Beneath the stars, we dare believe,
Love's palette leads us in dance.

Moments captured in soft sighs,
Echoes of a fleeting time.
With every heartbeat, hope complies,
In artistry, our hearts rhyme.

Through the shades of joy and pain,
We find strength within our years.
In the heart, love's true refrain,
Painted bold, yet soft with tears.

Scarlet Chronicles

Once upon a crimson sky,
Where the shadows softly creep.
Stories woven, unsure why,
Secrets held that dare not sleep.

Each page turned holds echoes clear,
Of laughter lost, and dreams reclaimed.
With every drop of crimson fear,
A tale of love, forever framed.

Blood and wine, a bittersweet,
Moments tangled, hearts collide.
In the silence, stories meet,
Where agony and joy reside.

Fleeting glances, passions flare,
In the depth of evening's glow.
Scarlet threads intertwine with care,
Marking paths we dared to go.

As the dawn begins to rise,
Fading whispers fade from sight.
In the heart, the truth still lies,
Scarlet chronicles, our light.

A Stitch in Time

In the fabric of our days,
Moments stitched with hopes and dreams.
Through the haze, life's winding ways,
Each thread tells a tale, it seems.

Time's gentle hands, they weave and pull,
Tapestries of joy and pain.
With each stitch, our hearts are full,
Mending paths, through loss and gain.

Stitch by stitch, the memories form,
An intricate dance of fate.
Through the calm and through the storm,
Every patch we sew, creates.

In the seams where laughter lies,
We find solace, love's embrace.
A tapestry beneath the skies,
Each thread connecting, time and space.

As we gather, day by day,
The fabric of our lives makes sense.
A stitch in time, come what may,
Binding our hearts, it's all immense.

The Veil of Vermilion

Beneath the veil of twilight's shade,
Crimson whispers softly rise.
In silence, stories sweetly laid,
Wrapped in dreams, our hearts surprise.

In vermilion, the sun dips low,
Painting skies with passion's fire.
Each moment crafted, hearts in tow,
Awakening our deepest desires.

A veil drawn tight in evening's glow,
Hiding secrets wrapped in song.
As night unfolds, the time will show,
In vermilion, we all belong.

With every heartbeat, love's embrace,
In shades of red, emotions stir.
Through the veil, we find our place,
In sunsets where our spirits purr.

Beneath the stars, we dare to dream,
In vermilion's warm delight.
With every thread, our hopes redeem,
Veiled in passion, shining bright.

The Stitches of Fate

Threads of silver intertwined,
Each moment stitched in time.
We weave our hopes and dreams,
In the quiet, silent chime.

Paths crossed in a fleeting glance,
Destinies unraveled tight.
With every choice we dance,
Woven in the fabric of night.

A needle's prick, a gentle tug,
Each stitch a tale to tell.
In the tapestry, we snug,
Fate whispers its soft spell.

From frayed edges, strength is found,
In scars, our stories bloom.
Together, we are bound,
Creating beauty from the gloom.

So let us sew with all our heart,
Embroider what's yet to be.
In every seam, a work of art,
The stitches of fate set free.

A Tapestry of Passion

Threads of gold, a fiery hue,
Woven close in night's embrace.
Passion breathes and whispers true,
In this warm and tender space.

Silent glances, fingers trace,
Every fiber holds a sign.
Together we create our place,
In the rhythm, hearts align.

Colors blend in frantic rush,
Heartbeats thrum, a wild sound.
In this vivid, vibrant hush,
Our souls dance, forever bound.

Each moment fraught with desire,
Each stitch a spark, ignites our flame.
In the shadows, we conspire,
To write a love without a name.

Unraveled threads, yet never torn,
A tapestry of souls combined.
In this woven love reborn,
Eternally, our hearts entwined.

Scarlet Whispers

Crimson threads softly entwine,
Echoes linger in the air.
Whispers shared, a love divine,
In the twilight, bold and rare.

Secrets wrapped in velvet night,
Scarlet promises unfold.
In the shadows, passion's light,
A warmth that never grows old.

Hearts entwined in quiet song,
Each note a brush of fate.
In this dance, we both belong,
Scarlet whispers never wait.

Lingering in starlit dreams,
Kisses stolen in the dark.
Every glance and laugh redeems,
Igniting joy, a gentle spark.

So let the night embrace our love,
With every hue that tightly binds.
In each whisper, we rise above,
Scarlet threads of hearts and minds.

The Fabric of Desire

Woven deep in every glance,
A fabric rich and finely spun.
In this quiet, daring dance,
Our hearts beat as a single drum.

Threads of longing, soft and bold,
Each touch ignites the air around.
In silken layers, stories told,
Desire's flame in silence found.

Interwoven dreams take flight,
In the night, our souls collide.
From shadows, we emerge in light,
Two hearts on passion's endless tide.

With every sigh, we tie the knot,
A bond unbroken, strong and true.
In the fabric, we are caught,
In the weave, it's me and you.

So let us touch with gentle care,
Embroider all we hold so dear.
In the fabric of desire,
Let love's rich tapestry draw near.

Scarlet Memories Unraveled

In twilight's glow, the shadows dance,
Whispered secrets, lost in a trance.
Fragments of laughter linger near,
Carved in the heart, forever clear.

Amidst the roses, a memory blooms,
Petals unfold, dispelling the glooms.
A crimson hue paints the darkened skies,
As time unwinds, the spirit flies.

Each sigh a thread, woven with care,
In the fabric of love, we lay bare.
Threads of the past entwine our fate,
In the tapestry bright, we navigate.

Echoes of joy, the warmth of grace,
In the gallery of dreams we embrace.
Through storms and sun, our journey flows,
Bound by the heart, where affection grows.

So let the memories softly shine,
Like stars that twinkle, forever divine.
Scarlet tales penned in the night,
Unraveled softly, in love's pure light.

The Kisses of Maraschino

In a garden sweet, where memories play,
Beneath the boughs, we drift and sway.
With every kiss, the world stands still,
Maraschino blooms, a cherry thrill.

Lips meet lips, a promise in bloom,
Sugary whispers, dispelling gloom.
In the hush of dusk, sweet nectar gleams,
As passion ignites the tender dreams.

Every touch dances, like petals in air,
Entwined together, a moment rare.
The taste of summer, so rich and bold,
A sweet serenade, a story told.

Through sunlit days and moonlit nights,
Our hearts entwined, in dazzling flights.
With kisses so sweet, love blooms anew,
Maraschino moments, just me and you.

With laughter that sparkles, joy that sings,
In the warmth of love, the heart takes wing.
A journey of flavors, forever bestowed,
In kisses of maraschino, our love flowed.

Weave of Eternal Flame

From embers born, the fire ignites,
With every breath, pure passion delights.
Threads of desire, entwined so tight,
In the glow of the stars, we unite.

Fingers dance, tracing heartbeats' song,
A flame that flickers, where we belong.
A tapestry woven, rich and profound,
In the quiet moments, love is found.

Through trials faced, our spirits soar,
In the weave of flames, we crave for more.
Every spark whispers, secrets shared,
Binding our souls, forever paired.

In the warmth of night, our shadows blend,
No beginning or end, just time to spend.
The eternal flame, a guiding light,
Together we burn, in love's pure flight.

With every flicker, our story unfolds,
In the weave of eternal flame, love holds.
A dance of hearts, forever embraced,
In the warmth of the fire, our dreams are laced.

Threads between Souls

In the quiet hush, threads softly weave,
Connecting the hearts that dare to believe.
Invisible ties, binding us close,
In the tapestry of life, love's sweet prose.

Across the vastness, where silence sings,
A bond unbroken, the comfort it brings.
Through joy and sorrow, we stand as one,
Threads intertwine, our journey begun.

With every heartbeat, a story unfolds,
In whispers of warmth, the truth gently molds.
Across the ages, our spirits entwine,
In the threads between souls, there's a sign.

Through the storms we weather, side by side,
In the tapestry of love, we abide.
Rooted in trust, anchored in grace,
Each thread a promise, no time can erase.

The fabric of dreams, stitched with care,
In every moment, love's essence laid bare.
Threads of our souls, eternally spun,
In this grand design, we are forever one.

Weaving Dreams in Garnet

In a world of deep desire,
We weave our dreams on threads of fire.
Stars twinkle like garnets bright,
Guiding us through the velvet night.

Whispers dance on the evening breeze,
Carried softly through the ancient trees.
Each heartbeat reflects the glow,
A tapestry of hopes that we sow.

Colors blend in a gentle swirl,
As thoughts and wishes begin to unfurl.
With every stitch, we draw near,
Creating magic crafted from fear.

Through the shadows, shadows play,
Garnet dreams will light our way.
In the silence, visions bloom,
Filling every corner of the room.

We gather strength from the night sky,
Learning to reach, learning to fly.
With threads of garnet, we rise and gleam,
Sewing together our wildest dream.

The Scarlet Songbird

In the dawn, a songbird sings,
With notes as bright as summer's wings.
Crimson feathers catch the light,
Painting mornings pure and bright.

With every chirp, a tale unfolds,
Of love and loss, of dreams untold.
Across the meadow, free and proud,
The scarlet songbird draws a crowd.

Echoes linger in the air,
A melody beyond compare.
In the twilight, its voice remains,
Whispering softly through the plains.

When shadows fall, it takes to flight,
Leaving behind the fading light.
Yet every note still echoes clear,
The songbird's heart is always near.

Nestled in the branches high,
With every tune, we learn to fly.
The scarlet songbird, bold and free,
A symbol of our harmony.

Ties of Ruby

Through the ages, bonds are made,
In the warmth of a heart that won't fade.
Ruby ties hold us near,
In laughter shared and every tear.

Moments strung like pearls of light,
Each memory a joyous sight.
With hands entwined, we face the storm,
In ruby warmth, we stay warm.

Time may wander, yet we stay,
Tied together, come what may.
With every thread, our tales are spun,
In the dance of life, we are one.

Through trials fierce, we bravely stand,
With ruby ties that understand.
As seasons change and rivers flow,
Our bond grows stronger, this we know.

Years will pass, yet love remains,
Anchored deep through joys and pains.
Though the world may shift and sway,
Our ties of ruby will not fray.

Threads of Emotion

In the fabric of our days,
Threads of emotion weave through the gray.
Joy and sorrow, laughter and sighs,
Stitch our stories, bind our ties.

Colorful strands of vibrant hues,
Paint our hearts with every bruise.
Woven tight, yet free to roam,
Each thread a pulse of love and home.

Patterns shift as seasons change,
Life's rich tapestry can rearrange.
With delicate hands, we sew and mend,
Creating beauty that won't end.

Amidst the chaos, threads hold tight,
Through darkest hours, they shine bright.
An embrace of fibers soft and strong,
Guiding us where we belong.

In each stitch, a tale we write,
Threads of emotion, day and night.
May our fabric never wear thin,
For in love's weave, we always win.

Echoes of Vermilion

Whispers dance in fading light,
Memories linger in the night.
Vermilion skies of dreams unspun,
Echoes stir, for we are one.

Footsteps trace the path of fire,
Hearts entwined in soft desire.
Every glance, a tale retold,
Woven threads of crimson gold.

Time stands still beneath the trees,
Caught in moments, like a breeze.
Vermilion leaves, they turn and glide,
Holding secrets, deep inside.

Shadows play in twilight's glow,
Silent stories, ebb and flow.
In the stillness, voices sigh,
Echoes linger, never die.

As day surrenders to the night,
Vermilion dreams take flight.
With every heartbeat, every breath,
Life's tapestry weaves through death.

Stitches of Memory

Threads of time, so tightly sewn,
In every stitch, a heart is known.
Memories fade yet softly cling,
Whispers of what the past will bring.

Fabric worn, but colors bright,
Stitched together in the night.
Every tear, a story told,
Stitches mended, brave and bold.

Hands that sew with love and care,
Binding moments that we share.
Time's embrace, a gentle span,
Stitches of memory, where we stand.

Patchwork dreams in life's design,
Each fragment, a cherished line.
Tales entwined, forever cast,
Stitches holding moments fast.

With every knot, the bond grows tight,
Sewn in shadows, caught in light.
Embroidered dreams that never stray,
In stitches of memory, we stay.

A Dance in Crimson

Crimson petals fall like rain,
Whirling softly, joy and pain.
Dancing under the moon's embrace,
Life's sweet rhythm, a tender grace.

Figures twirl in twilight's haze,
Caught in echoes of golden days.
Every step, a breath of fire,
Heartbeats match a wild desire.

A dance that stirs the ancient ground,
Notes of passion swirl around.
Spinning dreams in vibrant hue,
Where the world feels fresh and new.

In the shadows, secrets weave,
Crimson threads that never leave.
In each movement, stories grow,
A dance in crimson, soft and slow.

When dawn breaks, the dance must cease,
Yet in our hearts, a perfect piece.
Bound together in life's delight,
A dance persists, day and night.

Tyd in Outrage

Beneath the weight of silent cries,
Fractured hopes in darkened skies.
Voices rise in stormy air,
Tyd in outrage, stripped and bare.

Fires burn in the hearts of few,
Fury rising, fierce and true.
The world awakens to the call,
Together standing, never small.

Chains once strong are worn and weak,
Courage found in those who speak.
Time for change, a time to fight,
Tyd in outrage, hearts ignite.

Echoes of the past still haunt,
Yet in defiance, spirits flaunt.
From ashes rise a brighter day,
In outrage, we find our way.

With every heartbeat, strength renewed,
In darkness, seeds of hope are brewed.
Though winds may howl, we claim our ground,
Tyd in outrage, fiercely bound.

Echoes of Sanguine Dreams

In twilight's hug, shadows play,
Whispers of hopes, drift away.
Fleeting glimmers in the night,
Softly glow, the heart's delight.

Every sigh, a gentle stream,
Carrying forth, a tender dream.
An embrace of starlit grace,
In solace, we find our place.

Echoes dance on the moonbeam's arc,
Softly calling from the dark.
With each pulse, lost things revive,
In these dreams, we feel alive.

Time, a wisp, slips like sand,
Holding tight, a helping hand.
In the stillness, secrets bloom,
Awakening in this room.

At dawn, when dreams start to fade,
The heart knows not to be afraid.
For in each echo, love will soar,
Sanguine dreams, forever more.

Crimson Strokes on Canvas

A brush in hand, the colors blend,
Crimson whispers, the stories send.
Each stroke a rhythm, wild and free,
On the canvas, hearts can see.

Heartbeat echoes in shades so bright,
Painting passions in soft twilight.
Vivid hues, a lover's glance,
Capturing life's fragile dance.

Cascades of red, with splashes bold,
Tales of warmth, eternally told.
Beneath the surface, secrets flow,
In every layer, emotions grow.

Time stands still in a painter's gaze,
Lost in strokes of a vibrant haze.
As shadows mingle with the light,
Art creates a world so bright.

The canvas holds our dreams and fears,
Each crimson hue, a trail of tears.
But in beauty, we find our might,
Crimson strokes, a radiant sight.

Ties of Ruby

In a garden where roses grow,
Threads of ruby, softly glow.
Binding hearts in endless grace,
Whispers linger in this space.

Ties of ruby, warm and bright,
Drawing closer, day and night.
In every petal, love is found,
Entwined souls, forever bound.

Through storms and skies of fragile blue,
The ties of ruby see us through.
With every touch, a promise made,
In the silence, bonds don't fade.

Glance by glance, the world will fade,
With each heartbeat, love cascades.
Against the tides, we hold on tight,
Our ruby ties, a beacon's light.

Moments treasured, like the dawn,
In this dance, we've always drawn.
Through every trial, love will steer,
Ties of ruby, crystal clear.

The Velvet Connection

In hush of night, soft whispers blend,
Velvet threads, the heart does mend.
A gentle touch, comfort wraps tight,
In silence, we find our light.

The warmth of dreams in every seam,
Weave together, like tender beams.
Each glance a spark, igniting flames,
In this bond, we share our names.

Through shadows deep, and paths unknown,
The velvet connection has grown.
Holding tightly, the world stands still,
In a dance of fate, we fulfill.

Like morning dew on petals rare,
This love, a treasure, beyond compare.
Embracing whispers, so profound,
In velvet comfort, we are found.

Each heartbeat sings a melody sweet,
Life's symphony, when souls meet.
In every moment, love reflects,
In velvet dreams, no regrets.

Threads of Warmth

In the quiet of the night,
Whispers soft, feelings bright,
Wrapped in dreams, we intertwine,
Threads of warmth, your heart is mine.

Through the storms, we find our way,
Hand in hand, come what may,
Stitches tight, the fabric strong,
Together where we both belong.

With each laugh, we weave our tale,
In every sorrow, we prevail,
Colors blend, and hearts align,
Threads of warmth, forever shine.

In the echoes, love will stay,
Guiding us, come what may,
Underneath the starlit sky,
With each thread, we learn to fly.

So here's to us, in life's embrace,
Finding strength in every trace,
Through every moment, night and day,
Threads of warmth will lead the way.

A Stitch in Flame

With a spark that ignites the night,
A stitch in flame, burning bright,
Passion dances like a fawn,
In a world where dreams are drawn.

Through the shadows, flame persists,
In the silence, love exists,
Sewing hearts with threads of fire,
A tapestry that never tires.

Moments flicker, memories burn,
In the fabric, lessons learned,
With each stitch, we build our dream,
A stitch in flame, a blazing beam.

In the embers, hope remains,
Lighting pathways, breaking chains,
Through the years, this fire grows,
A stitch in flame, forever glows.

So take my hand, let's breathe the night,
With every thread, we'll find our light,
Together weaving fate's grand plan,
A stitch in flame, where love began.

Claret Cascade

Crimson rivers gently flow,
In the garden where dreams sow,
Claret cascade, soft and sweet,
Nature's bounty at our feet.

Petals blush in the sun's embrace,
Each drop holds a secret place,
Where laughter mingles with the dusk,
In claret hues, we feel the rush.

Gather 'round the flowing stream,
Life's rich tapestry, a dream,
With every sip, we taste delight,
Claret cascade in the fading light.

Here in twilight, shadows dance,
Spinning tales of love and chance,
Each moment shared, a cherished blend,
Claret cascade, where stories bend.

So lift your glass and toast the day,
To the beauty that won't decay,
In this river, we'll forever wade,
Claret cascade, memories made.

The Laces of Love

With every tie, our hearts entwined,
In the fabric of the kind,
The laces of love hold us near,
Binding dreams, dismissing fear.

Step by step, we journey on,
In the dusk before the dawn,
Each knot a promise, firm and true,
The laces of love, me and you.

Through the trials and the cheer,
Every whisper, every tear,
We lace our stories, stitch by stitch,
In this love, we find our niche.

Threads of laughter, shades of pain,
In the sunshine, in the rain,
As we walk through life's embrace,
The laces of love, our sacred space.

So let us dance, let's paint the night,
In our hearts, a shining light,
These laces, woven, never part,
The laces of love, one beating heart.

The Ribbon of Moments

Time weaves a soft thread,
In colors bright and bold.
Each moment a whisper,
A story yet untold.

Joy dances in sunlight,
While shadows play their part.
Memories glide on by,
Captured in the heart.

Laughter echoes sweetly,
In the corners of the mind.
Embraced by gentle breezes,
In the moments we find.

Threads of love entwined,
In a tapestry of dreams.
Each stitch a connection,
In the flow of our themes.

So hold tight those moments,
Let them shimmer and shine.
For in life's fleeting dance,
Each second is divine.

Intricate Paths in Cherry

Under blossoms so bright,
Paths meander and twine.
Whispers in the branches,
A promise in each line.

Soft petals touch the ground,
Painting stories anew.
In the heart of the orchard,
Life's beauty breaks through.

A labyrinth of laughter,
In the vibrant spring air.
Footsteps mark the journey,
In shades beyond compare.

Shadows play with the light,
As the sun dips and dives.
Each corner a secret,
Where adventure thrives.

So stroll through the pathways,
Take a moment to see.
The intricate weavings,
Of cherry, you and me.

A Mosaic of Heart Finds

In the gallery of dreams,
Each piece tells a tale.
Colors blend and collide,
In the heart's gentle veil.

Fragments of laughter,
And tears in soft hues.
Crafted by the moments,
In the path that we choose.

Every shape a whisper,
A journey carved in time.
The whispers tell stories,
In rhythm and rhyme.

With patience and love,
We create our design.
Each shard a reminder,
Of bright stars that align.

Together, we build it,
A masterpiece divine.
In the mosaic of heart finds,
Our souls intertwine.

The Flame Forged in Red

In the ember's warm glow,
Passion ignites the night.
A blaze of fierce longing,
Filling shadows with light.

Through struggles and trials,
Our spirits intertwine.
With every spark we find,
A strength so divine.

Hearts beating like drums,
In the rhythm of fire.
Each flicker a promise,
To lift us up higher.

Together we dance,
In the warmth of our trust.
A flame forged in red,
In love's sacred dust.

So let the fire roar,
In the night's fierce embrace.
For the flame that we kindle,
Is our timeless grace.

Garnet Fables

In the quiet of the night,
Garnet dreams take flight,
Whispers dance on moonlit air,
Tales woven with tender care.

Underneath the ancient trees,
Stories drift like autumn leaves,
Glimmers of a past replete,
Where love and loss softly meet.

A river flows with secret songs,
In harmony, where hope belongs,
Fables etched in stones will stay,
Guarding memories along the way.

Crimson hues in every glance,
Invite the heart to take a chance,
As shadows linger on the ground,
In garnet dreams, joy is found.

The Restless Silk

Threaded tales of whispers bold,
In restless silk, the stories unfold,
Alive with colors, vivid and bright,
Woven in the seams of night.

Every stitch a heart's desire,
Patterns dance like flickering fire,
Embroidered hopes in shadows cast,
Embrace the future, forget the past.

Silken breezes sweep the land,
Carrying dreams, as soft as sand,
Beneath the stars, we find our way,
In the fabric of a new dawn's day.

Threads of fate entwined as one,
Across the world, the dreams have spun,
In restless silk, we strive to weave,
Our stories live, and we believe.

Connections in Coral

Beneath the waves, a world we find,
Connections made, hearts intertwined,
Coral castles, vibrant and grand,
Nature's artistry, hand in hand.

Whispers of the ocean's song,
In every tide, we belong,
A symphony of life at sea,
In coral reefs, we find our glee.

Colors burst in radiant spree,
Where sea and sky hold secrets free,
In every nook, life's treasures hide,
Connections in coral, side by side.

Together we dance, release our fears,
Riding the waves, through laughter and tears,
In the embrace of the ocean wide,
In coral depths, our souls collide.

The Warmth of Sunset Shadows

As day says farewell, colors blend,
The warmth of shadows starts to send,
A gentle hush blankets the land,
With whispers soft, like a lover's hand.

Golden rays drip from the sky,
Painting dreams as the sun waves goodbye,
Night's embrace draws ever near,
In sunset's glow, we lose our fear.

The horizon holds secrets untold,
In twilight's arms, we grow bold,
Each fading hue a memory dear,
In the warm shadows, love draws near.

When stars awaken, the dance begins,
In the night's soft touch, our story spins,
The warmth of sunset shadows blend,
In twilight dreams, together we mend.

The Journey of Ruby Paths

Through winding trails the ruby shines,
Each step whispers of ancient signs.
Beneath the gaze of starlit night,
We wander onward, hearts alight.

In valleys deep, with hopes to soar,
The paths unfold, revealing more.
The echoing secrets of the land,
Guide us gently, hand in hand.

Each bump and bend tells tales of old,
A tapestry of courage bold.
As we tread softly, dreams ignite,
In the glow of the fading light.

With ruby hues that paint the sky,
We find our truth, we learn to fly.
Through every shade, love's warmth will grow,
Onward, dear friend, together we go.

The journey ends not in despair,
But blossoms forth in vibrant air.
With ruby paths that always gleam,
We find our way, we chase the dream.

Unraveling Truths

In whispers soft, the truths unfold,
Like petals rich in tales retold.
We seek the heart beneath the lies,
A world awash with silent cries.

Each question asked reveals a thread,
Of stories penned, and words unsaid.
As shadows dance, the light draws near,
We find in pain, a voice so clear.

Unraveling knots of twisted fate,
We dare to seek, we dare to wait.
In the silence, wisdom's song,
Reminds us where our hearts belong.

Through valleys deep, we wander far,
Guided by the evening star.
With every step, a truth we claim,
In the tapestry of hope, we name.

United in this quest for light,
We lift our heads to face the night.
Unraveling veils, setting free,
The truths that bind, that let us be.

The Colors of Connection

In vibrant hues, our souls align,
A spectrum bright, a love divine.
Through every shade, we intertwine,
In colors bold, our hearts combine.

Blues of calm and greens of grace,
Create a world, a warm embrace.
With every laugh, a crimson spark,
Illuminating the shadowed dark.

Together we paint the canvas bright,
With strokes of joy and pure delight.
In every hue, a story told,
Of bonds that bloom, of hearts so bold.

The colors dance, a symphony,
A melody of unity.
In every clash, a moment gleams,
Reflecting hopes, embracing dreams.

Together rooted, side by side,
In this mosaic, we take pride.
In the colors of connection near,
We find our strength, we conquer fear.

Garnet Dreams

Deep in the night, the garnets gleam,
Whispers of fate; they softly dream.
With every glint, a wish takes flight,
Guided by hope, we chase the light.

In shadows long, where silence sings,
Garnet visions bring forth new wings.
Each pulse a beat, each thought a spark,
Illuminating the unknown dark.

Within the depths, true treasure lies,
Wrapped in courage, under skies.
As dawn breaks through, the dreams awaken,
In radiant paths, we are unshaken.

The journey calls, with garlands bright,
Garnet dreams guide our flight.
Through every challenge, we will find,
The treasures of the heart and mind.

Hand in hand, we dance and sway,
In a garden where dreams hold sway.
Together we'll weave our destiny,
Through garnet dreams, we will be free.

The Knot of Fate

In shadows deep, our paths entwine,
Threads of time in patterns divine,
Each choice we make, a stitch so tight,
Woven together, hearts take flight.

Fate's gentle hands, they pull and weave,
In moments fleeting, we believe,
The ties we form, they bend and sway,
Guiding us in a mystic ballet.

Signs of the stars, the moon's soft glow,
Charting our course, where will we go?
With every twist, our stories blend,
In this great dance, we shall transcend.

Each thread a whisper, a tale of old,
Of love and loss, and dreams untold,
In the loom of life, we find our place,
As we navigate this boundless space.

Together we stand, despite the storm,
In this tapestry, our hearts have worn,
We'll hold the past, embrace the new,
In the Knot of Fate, it's me and you.

Scarlet Cahoots

In the glow of dawn, secrets gleam,
Whispers of lovers, a daring dream,
Silken ties in shades of red,
Together we dance, where few dare tread.

Paths unbeknownst, we took our chance,
With hearts afire, a fervent dance,
Hand in hand, through shadows we glide,
In Scarlet Cahoots, our spirits collide.

Glimmers of hope, the night's sweet sigh,
Under starlit skies, just you and I,
Veils of twilight, drawn close and tight,
In every embrace, our passions ignite.

Fleeting moments, yet timeless remain,
In laughter and tears, we feel the pain,
Fractured memories, patched with grace,
Bound by the colors of love's embrace.

Together we rise, together we fall,
In this fervid tale, we'll give it our all,
For in the chaos, our bond stays true,
In Scarlet Cahoots, it's me and you.

Interwoven Destinies

Threads of life in colors wide,
Each moment shared, with hearts as guide,
In the fabric of time, our fates align,
Interwoven Destinies, a tapestry fine.

Sunlit days and stormy nights,
In shadows cast, we find our lights,
With every step, we twine and spin,
A journey taken, where dreams begin.

Life's intricate weave, a delicate art,
Stitch by stitch, we craft our part,
In tangled knots, we find our way,
Through trials faced, come what may.

Moments fleeting, yet forever we hold,
Stories reborn, in whispers told,
In the loom of fate, our spirits soar,
Bound by the love we can't ignore.

Together as one, we'll face the test,
In this grand scheme, our hearts at rest,
For in the weave of life's embrace,
Interwoven Destinies, through time and space.

The Whisper of Rubies

Beneath the stars, secrets do play,
In twilight's glow, we find our way,
Softly spoken, a tender breath,
The Whisper of Rubies, life intertwined with death.

Glistening treasures in shadows stay,
Each precious moment, a chance to sway,
Hearts pounding like drums, fierce and true,
In silken whispers, our love renews.

Ruby lips, a promise made,
Against the night, we aren't afraid,
Our hands entwined, unbreakable bond,
In the hush of darkness, our hearts respond.

Through storms we've traveled, still we shine,
Each cut and bruise, a sign divine,
With every heartbeat, we navigate,
For the joy we've found, we celebrate.

Together, we'll write love's endless song,
Through whispers sweet, where we belong,
In the tapestry of dreams, our love probes,
The Whisper of Rubies, a treasure that glows.

The Red River Runs

The river flows with a gentle grace,
Beneath the sky's vast embrace.
Whispers of stories, old and deep,
In currents where memories sleep.

Through mountains tall and valleys wide,
The red river flows, a silent guide.
It dances with shadows, it sparkles and gleams,
Carrying forth the heart's quiet dreams.

It cradles the valleys in its soft embrace,
Reflecting the stars, heaven's face.
A lifeline woven through time and space,
In its depths, the world's heartbeat we trace.

With each twist and turn, it sings a song,
Of love and loss, where we belong.
The echoes of laughter, the tears we've shed,
In the red river's heart, our secrets are fed.

So let us wander where the river flows,
Where the journey begins, and the magic glows.
For in its waters, we come alive,
With the red river's pulse, our spirits thrive.

Weaving the Unseen

Threads of life in colors bright,
Woven together, day and night.
In patterns complex, they intertwine,
Creating a fabric, yours and mine.

Each thread a story, a moment caught,
In the loom of existence, wisdom sought.
From laughter to sorrow, joy to grief,
We weave our tales, both wild and brief.

The unseen hands guide us along,
In the rhythm of life, we find our song.
With every knot that binds us tight,
We embrace the shadows, seeking the light.

Through vibrant hues and textures rare,
The tapestry grows, beyond compare.
Unraveling dreams in the silence profound,
In the weave of the unseen, our souls are found.

So let us cherish each intricate thread,
In the grand design where we are led.
For life's rich fabric, diverse and free,
Holds the beauty of you and me.

Smile of a Scarlet Sunrise

The dawn breaks forth in scarlet hue,
Awakening dreams, fresh and new.
Golden rays spill across the land,
Painting the world with nature's hand.

The whispers of morning begin to rise,
Under the gaze of brightening skies.
Birds chirp sweetly, a joyful tune,
In harmony with the waking moon.

With each passing moment, colors ignite,
Casting shadows that dance in the light.
A promise renewed with every ray,
The smile of dawn chasing night away.

In the silence of morning, hearts align,
As the world breathes in, a sacred sign.
Hope blooms brightly as day breaks free,
Wrapped in the warmth of possibility.

So rise with the sun, embrace the day,
With the smile of a scarlet sunrise, find your way.
Let the beauty of morning guide you near,
In the landscapes of dreams, let go of fear.

The Tapestry of Life

In threads of time, our stories blend,
A tapestry woven with love to send.
Each color a moment, precious and rare,
In the fabric of life, we find our care.

We stitch our dreams with hope and grace,
In every heartbeat, every embrace.
With laughter that dances and tears that fall,
We create a design, a universal call.

Through trials faced and mountains climbed,
In every stitch, our spirits chimed.
With hands outstretched, we lift each other,
In the grand tapestry, sister and brother.

Embroidered with memories, joys, and strife,
Together we weave the essence of life.
In intricate patterns, our hearts align,
Creating a beauty that continues to shine.

So cherish each thread, both weak and strong,
In the tapestry of life, we all belong.
For in this great weave, we share the light,
A masterpiece glowing, forever bright.

Crimson Weavings

In twilight's glow, threads intertwine,
Stitched by the hands of fate divine.
A tale unfolds in shades of red,
Where love and longing dare to tread.

Beneath the stars, secrets are spun,
Crimson tales of two, now one.
With every knot, a promise made,
In woven dreams, hearts are laid.

A dance of shadows, a gleam of light,
In every corner, passion's flight.
The loom's embrace, a gentle sway,
Crimson weavings will never fray.

Whispers of joy, and sighs of pain,
Through every thread, we stake our claim.
A tapestry rich, where sorrows blend,
In crimson weavings, we find our mend.

So let the fabric hold our soul,
In every stitch, we feel the whole.
Together we stand, come what may,
In this crimson weaving, forever stay.

Scarlet Whispers

Beneath the moon, whispers arise,
Carried softly through midnight skies.
Scarlet secrets in shadows play,
Echoes of love that never sway.

A heart unveiled, in passion's breath,
Drawing closer, defying death.
Lips that tremble, words unspoken,
In every glance, a bond unbroken.

Tender moments in fading light,
Scarlet hues paint stories bright.
With every heartbeat, time suspends,
A dance of souls that never ends.

Soft caress of a lover's sigh,
In crimson dusk where spirits lie.
Scarlet whispers on the breeze,
A melody that brings us ease.

So let us linger, lost in dreams,
Where love flows like gentle streams.
In the embrace of night's gentle grip,
We find our truth in scarlet script.

Tapestry of Ember

Flickering flames in the quiet night,
A tapestry woven with ember's light.
Each thread a story, caught in the glow,
Of passion's dance, we come to know.

In every spark, a memory burned,
Lessons of love, and hearts that turned.
The warmth that lingers, the heat that stays,
In a tapestry of ember, we find our ways.

Intricacies formed in shadows' play,
Colors entwined, come what may.
With every flame, we rise and fall,
Tapestry of ember, binding us all.

Through trials faced and dreams embraced,
A molten bond that can't be replaced.
In flickers of fire, our truths are found,
In tapestry of ember, love knows no bound.

So through the night, we weave our fate,
With hands entwined, we celebrate.
A glowing fabric, stitched with care,
In tapestry of ember, hearts laid bare.

Stitches of Passion

With needle pointed and fervent flame,
We sew the fabric, call love by name.
Stitches of passion, fiercely sewn,
In the heart's embrace, we have grown.

Each thread a promise, soft and tight,
Binding us closer, with pure delight.
In every loop, our dreams align,
Stitches of passion, you are mine.

Through trials faced, we rise anew,
In every scar, a story true.
With every stitch, our souls remain,
Ties that bind through joy and pain.

As twilight descends and shadows dance,
We find our rhythm in a shared romance.
In fabric's warmth, we lose control,
Stitches of passion, weaving our soul.

So let us craft this love we share,
In gentle touch, in whispered air.
For in these stitches, hearts we fashion,
A tapestry bright, of stitches of passion.

Soulful Stitches

In the quiet of the night,
Threads of silver glow so bright.
Whispers from the heart entreat,
Stitching dreams in rhythm sweet.

Each stitch holds a tale so dear,
Beneath the fabric, love draws near.
Colors woven, deep and bold,
Every secret waiting to unfold.

Patterns dance like shadows near,
Embroidered hopes, a tapestry clear.
With needle's grace and gentle hand,
We craft our world, so finely planned.

Life a quilt, both warm and worn,
Sewn together, spirits reborn.
In every patch, a faded smile,
A journey shared, a winding mile.

In each embrace, a story sews,
Binds us gently, love bestows.
Soulful stitches, heartbeats blend,
A masterpiece, our lives commend.

The Call of the Scarlet Life

Beneath the glow of twilight skies,
A fierce desire, a fire flies.
The world awakens, colors bloom,
In scarlet shades, we find our room.

Whispers echo from the past,
In every heartbeat, shadows cast.
Life's adventure calls our name,
In crimson hues, we stake our claim.

With every dawn, the promise sings,
Of passion's flight on painted wings.
Emerging bold, the spirit twirls,
Embracing life, as magic unfurls.

Dancers weave in rhythmic grace,
In scarlet tints, find their place.
An anthem rises, fierce and true,
The call of life, forever new.

Let colors guide our every move,
In the scarlet life, we find our groove.
Together, singing, hearts alight,
In vibrant days and endless night.

Woven Threads of Memory

In the corners of my mind,
Woven threads of truth, I find.
Each moment captured, fragile strands,
Stories held in gentle hands.

Think of laughter, bittersweet,
Echoes linger in heartbeats.
Colors deep and textures bold,
Memories crafted, tales retold.

Time's embrace, a tapestry,
Weaving ages, you and me.
In every thread, a life once spun,
A soft reminder of love begun.

These fibers strong, yet fragile too,
Holding whispers, old and new.
In every stitch, a promise grows,
Woven threads of life, it shows.

Let us dance on time's vast loom,
Creating beauty to dispel gloom.
In memory's quilt, we rest tonight,
In woven threads, we find our light.

A Crimson Dreamscape

In the twilight, a dream takes flight,
A canvas painted in crimson light.
Whispers drift on the evening breeze,
In this dreamscape, hearts find ease.

Mountains rise in shades of red,
Where fantasies and wishes tread.
Stars twinkle like distant hopes,
In the night, our spirit copes.

With every breath, the vision blooms,
In crimson skies, dispelling glooms.
Each heartbeat echoes in the night,
As we dance in pure delight.

Through meadows vast, we wander free,
In this landscape, just you and me.
A world where magic softly gleams,
In the fabric of our dreams.

Awakened by the morning's song,
Our spirits soar, where we belong.
In a crimson dreamscape, hold me close,
Together weaving love's sweet prose.

The Olympian embroideries

Threads of gold in twilight spun,
Heroes dance beneath the sun.
Mountains whisper tales of yore,
Where legends linger evermore.

Silks of dreams entwined with fate,
In the halls of gods, we wait.
Each stitch a story, richly told,
Woven paths of brave and bold.

Temples rise with majesty,
Adorned in myths of victory.
A tapestry of strength and pride,
In every heart, the dreams abide.

As echoes of the past resound,
In every thread, our hopes are bound.
The loom of life, where visions play,
Enshrined in colors, night and day.

On Olympus, where stars awake,
Crafting worlds with every quake.
The embroideries of the sky,
In exalted beauty, we rely.

Weaving the Night in Crimson

Night descends with velvet grace,
A tapestry, a sacred space.
Crimson threads of twilight glow,
Weave the dreams we dare to sow.

Stars are stitched in darkened hues,
Whispers of forgotten views.
In this quilt, our hopes reside,
Where shadows and the dawn collide.

Moonlit rivers gently sway,
Guiding hearts who lose their way.
In the fabric of the night,
Crimson hues turn dark to light.

Patterns shift like fleeting time,
In the silence, hear the chime.
Each moment sewn with tender care,
A plush embrace, the night's affair.

As dawn approaches, softly near,
We treasure each moment dear.
In the loom where dreams take flight,
Forever weaving through the night.

Ties that Bleed

Bound by threads of pain and love,
Intertwined like stars above.
With each heartbeat, shadows cast,
Unraveled secrets of the past.

Chains that weave, yet pull apart,
Ties that bind the aching heart.
In every tear, a story told,
A tapestry of hues and gold.

Fading scars that mark the skin,
Testaments to where we've been.
Each knot a lesson, tight and bold,
A woven truth that must unfold.

In gentle hands, the threads unwind,
Exposing wounds we leave behind.
Yet with each stitch, we find our grace,
Reviving dreams we dare embrace.

Though ties may bleed and hearts may ache,
In every fracture, love awakes.
A fabric rich with life's decree,
For every tie can set us free.

A Symphony of Sienna

In the cradle of the land,
Where sienna takes a stand.
Golden fields, the sun's caress,
Nature's art, a soft finesse.

Rustling leaves and whispered air,
Every note, a vibrant flare.
Symphonies of earth and sky,
Harmonious, they softly sigh.

Brushstrokes dance on canvas wide,
In every hue, our dreams abide.
From dusk to dawn, our hearts align,
In this symphony divine.

As shadows weave through twilight's seam,
Echoes cradle every dream.
Notes of amber, copper fire,
Each stroke ignites a soul's desire.

In the pastures, melodies rise,
With each color, love defies.
A symphony of joy and pain,
In every moment, life's refrain.

A Symphony in Scarlet

Crimson leaves dance in the breeze,
A melody played on rustling trees.
Whispers of autumn fill the air,
Nature's palette, vibrant and rare.

Evening sun casts a golden hue,
A canvas painted in shades so true.
Each shadow lengthens, a gentle sigh,
As day bids farewell to the night sky.

Hearts beat to the rhythm of time,
In this moment, life feels sublime.
Scarlet hues ignite the soul's fire,
A symphony wrapped in deep desire.

Raindrops softly kiss the ground,
In every droplet, beauty is found.
The world exhales, fresh and anew,
In the symphony of scarlet hue.

With every heartbeat, love's sweet song,
In the twilight, we both belong.
Hand in hand, we chase the light,
A lasting promise in the night.

Vineyards of Blush

Rows of grapes under the sun,
Ripening fruits, the day is won.
In the breeze, sweet scents arise,
A whispering promise in twilight skies.

Beneath the leaves, shadows play,
As laughter dances, dusk turns gray.
Wine glasses clink, and spirits soar,
In vineyards of blush, we crave for more.

Crimson hues paint the evening fair,
With every sip, we lose our care.
Moments shared, a joyous spree,
In these vineyards, we're wild and free.

The earth is rich, the harvest near,
With each new season, love draws near.
From grape to glass, our dreams intertwine,
In this realm of luscious vine.

As stars appear, the night unfolds,
Stories of love, untold and bold.
In vineyards of blush, we find our way,
Embracing life, come what may.

The Heart's Loom

Threads of fate woven so tight,
In the tapestry, day turns to night.
Each color sings of dreams held dear,
The heart's loom whispers, love draws near.

Gentle hands guide the strands along,
In every twist lies a hidden song.
With patience and care, we stitch our tales,
In the quiet moments, love prevails.

Nature's hues bleed into one,
With every fiber, we come undone.
Intertwined in warmth and grace,
In the heart's loom, we find our place.

Through trials faced and joys embraced,
In every stitch, time's love is traced.
Bound together, we weave as one,
Inside this fabric, our hearts have spun.

With each passing season, we mend,
In the heart's loom, there's always a blend.
Tales of laughter, shadows, and light,
Our life's work shining in the night.

Twists of Vintage Wine

In dusty cellars, stories rest,
Each bottle whispers of its quest.
Twists of vintage, aged with time,
A dance of flavors, rich and sublime.

Cork pops softly, echoes ring,
In that moment, hearts take wing.
Dark red nectar, the glass reveals,
A tapestry woven of how it feels.

Savor the notes, so deep and bold,
Tales of summers, secrets told.
With every sip, a journey starts,
In twists of vintage, we share our hearts.

Time drips slowly like fine wine,
Memories swirl in a sacred line.
Life's moments captured, poured with grace,
In this elixir, we find our place.

As laughter flows, the night unwinds,
In the richness, solace we find.
With friends beside as we dine and toast,
In twists of vintage, we cherish most.

In the Shadows of Red

Whispers of dusk in crimson spread,
Beneath the moon where the heart is led.
Secrets linger in the twilight's glow,
Painting the night with an ember's flow.

A dance of shadows under starlit skies,
Where echoes of dreams softly arise.
Fires that flicker, gently entwined,
In the shadows, our souls aligned.

The tapestry woven of hues so deep,
Where passion stirs and memories seep.
Crimson tales that forever unfold,
In these shadows, our stories told.

With every heartbeat, the silence sings,
Wrapped in the warmth that a lost night brings.
In the shades of red, we find our way,
Through the silence that beckons to stay.

In the end, we shall rise anew,
In the embrace of this vibrant hue.
For in the shadows, love's fire remains,
Burning brightly through joys and pains.

The Poetic Weave of Indulgence

In every sip of the finest wine,
Moments gathered, hearts intertwine.
The laughter flows like a gentle stream,
In indulgence, we taste the dream.

Silken fabrics of sweet delight,
Unraveled stories in the quiet night.
Fleeting pleasures twinkling like stars,
Embracing beauty, forgetting the scars.

With each soft touch, a melody plays,
Crafting whispers in secret bays.
Wrapped in warmth of a lover's gaze,
In indulgent bliss, we softly graze.

Time bends gently, ever so slow,
In moments where passionate rivers flow.
The tides of desire gently swirl,
In the weave of our poetic world.

So raise a glass to the sweet embrace,
To the binding threads of this sacred space.
In indulgence, let us find our light,
As shadows dance through the velvet night.

Tinted Trails of Love

Beneath the arch of a painted sky,
We stroll together, hearts flying high.
With every step, new colors emerge,
On tinted trails where emotions surge.

Each path we wander, a story to tell,
In the hues of sunset, we cast our spell.
Hand in hand, through gardens we roam,
Find our solace, this love our home.

With the brush of fate, we color the day,
In love's sweet glow, we softly sway.
Moments captured in shades so bright,
In the canvas of joy, our hearts take flight.

As twilight settles, the stars align,
Ink of the night our dreams entwine.
In tinted trails, we leave our mark,
An indelible vein in the vibrant dark.

Embracing the journey, forever in sync,
With every heartbeat, we stop and think.
As love's brush paints the world anew,
In these tinted trails, it's just me and you.

Embered Heartstrings

In the quiet glow of a flickering fire,
Embered heartstrings pull ever higher.
With warmth and whispers, the night ignites,
Binding our souls in soft delights.

Each spark a promise, each flame a sigh,
In glowing coals, our spirits fly.
Love's gentle rhythm in the softest hum,
Comforting echoes of what's to come.

The dance of shadows sways with grace,
In the cradle of night, we find our place.
With eyes that shimmer like stars above,
In the embrace of the fire, we learn to love.

With every heartbeat, the ember's light,
Flickering softly, igniting the night.
In the warmth of passion, we willingly dive,
Through embered heartstrings, we come alive.

So let the fire burn bright and true,
In the silence, we feel love's hue.
Together forever, through thick and thin,
In the ember's glow, we let love in.

Patterns of the Heart

In shadows cast by soft moonlight,
The heart unveils its hidden art,
Each beat a dance, a whispered serenade,
Creating patterns, a work of heart.

Through joys and sorrows, it weaves and spins,
Threads of laughter, echoes of pain,
In every moment, a tapestry grows,
A map of feelings, loss, and gain.

With gentle hands, we trace each line,
Each pulse a story, a tale untold,
In rhythm's embrace, we find our way,
The patterns of love, both warm and bold.

In silence shared, in the chaos loud,
The heart remembers, it never forgets,
Fragments of joy and pieces of grief,
Intertwined in the dance of regrets.

So let us cherish this vivid design,
For patterns shift like the tides of the sea,
In every heart, a unique motif,
A symphony of life, wild and free.

Flickers of Sanguine

In the dawn's warm embrace, colors ignite,
A canvas painted with sanguine light,
Each flicker dances, a spark of desire,
Awakening dreams, setting hearts afire.

With whispers of passion, the day begins,
A melody soft, where hope never thins,
Through laughter and tears, the moments unfold,
Flickers of joy in hues bright and bold.

As twilight descends, the shadows entwine,
Echoing secrets we dare to define,
In every heartbeat, in each gentle sigh,
The sanguine flickers that never say die.

In the quiet of night, stars wink with glee,
Illuminating paths for the brave to foresee,
Each glimmer a promise, a wish softly made,
Flickers of sanguine in the glowing cascade.

So dance with the night, let your spirit soar,
In the flickering light, find what you adore,
For every fleeting moment holds magic inside,
Flickers of sanguine, in which we abide.

The Taste of Burgundy

In a glass swirls the ruby delight,
A cascade of flavors, rich and bright,
Each sip a journey through sun-kissed vine,
The taste of burgundy, bold and divine.

With notes of cherry and whispers of spice,
It beckons softly, encourages twice,
Moments savored, shared laughter and cheer,
The taste of burgundy, love drawing near.

As evening deepens, the stars take their place,
This potion of joy brings warmth to the space,
With stories exchanged, the cup overflows,
The taste of burgundy in twilight's glow.

In every drop, a memory lingers,
Of shared embraces and intertwining fingers,
With each toast raised, hearts open with glee,
The taste of burgundy, setting us free.

So let us indulge in this liquid embrace,
A dance upon tongues, a soft, sweet grace,
For in every bottle, romance we find,
The taste of burgundy, forever entwined.

Voices of the Scarlet Thread

In the quiet dusk, whispers entwine,
The voices of hearts, a tapestry divine,
Each thread a story, woven with care,
The scarlet thread sings of love laid bare.

Through valleys of laughter, and mountains of pain,
The voices rise up like a gentle refrain,
In harmony woven, in unison blend,
The scarlet thread holds what time cannot bend.

With echoes of passion, in shadows it flows,
Through moments that glimmer, where true love grows,
Each voice a reminder, a promise we keep,
The scarlet thread binds, in depths and in steep.

As dawn breaks anew, it carries our dreams,
The voices of hope in soft, flowing streams,
In colors so vivid, in warmth we connect,
The scarlet thread whispers of love's true effect.

So let us gather, in circles of light,
Where voices entwine, dispelling the night,
For in every heartbeat, every soul we thread,
The voices sing out, love's anthem widespread.

Fusion of Maroon

In the sunset's gentle haze,
Maroon whispers softly play,
Threads of dusk in warm embrace,
Nature's palette finds its grace.

Fires dance in evening's glow,
Heartbeats quicken as they flow,
Stitched together, hearts align,
In this fusion, love will shine.

Leaves of copper, skies of gold,
Stories of the brave retold,
Underneath the starry dome,
Through maroon, we find our home.

Waves of warmth in every seam,
Life a softly flowing stream,
Binding moments, treasures dear,
In maroon, we conquer fear.

Every stitch a tale to weave,
In this tapestry, believe,
Dancing shadows intertwined,
In the maroon, love defined.

The Crochet of Memories

In the corner, fibers rest,
Whispers of a time blessed,
Crocheted in moments shared,
Every loop, a life declared.

Yarns of laughter fill the air,
Tales of joy, a gentle snare,
Patterned hearts, each twist a dream,
Together strong, we find our theme.

Hands entwined, a loved one near,
Crafting warmth that draws us here,
In the stitches, stories blend,
Crochet binds, it will not bend.

Colors vibrant, memories bright,
Woven under moonlit night,
In every project, lessons learned,
With each thread, respect is earned.

From the past, we gather strength,
Lifetimes stretched, a woven length,
In this craft, a bond we find,
The crochet of hearts entwined.

Radiant Stitches

Fingers dance with vibrant thread,
Radiant patterns softly spread,
Every knot a spark of life,
Turning woes into delight.

Colors shine in radiant hues,
Crafted carefully, we choose,
In each stitch, a story grows,
In our hearts, the beauty flows.

From the fabric, dreams emerge,
Radiant energy, a surge,
With each twist, our hopes ignite,
In the canvas of the night.

Whispers soft of tales untold,
Woven warmth that we behold,
Hearts ablaze with radiant might,
In each stitch, we find the light.

Gather 'round this vibrant art,
Sew together, never part,
In our souls, the stitches gleam,
Radiant echoes of the dream.

The Chord of Crimson

In the twilight's deep embrace,
Crimson threads begin to trace,
Every heartbeat, every song,
Weaving tales that last so long.

Like a melody's sweet flow,
Crimson dreams begin to glow,
Harmony in every seam,
Lives entwined in one bright dream.

Softly strummed on heartstrings dear,
In this chord, we persevere,
Every note a story shared,
In the crimson, love declared.

Lively accents paint the air,
Colors rich, like love laid bare,
With each touch, our spirits rise,
Finding peace beneath the skies.

Echoes of the past invoke,
In this chord, the silence broke,
United in a crimson thread,
Together, where our hearts are led.

Flame's Embrace

In the heart of the night, a flicker ignites,
Whispers of warmth in the chill of the heights.
Dancing like shadows, they twist and they weave,
Carving sweet moments that tug at the sleeve.

A soft glow of passion, a burst, a delight,
Holding the echoes of dreams taking flight.
Embers reveal what the darkness conceals,
A tapestry woven with love's gentle wheels.

From ashes to sparks, our spirits collide,
With every embrace, we shed what we've tried.
In the flame's embrace, we find our own way,
Guided by glimmers that lead us to stay.

Together we linger, in this timeless dance,
Fueled by the warmth of a fleeting romance.
In the glow of desire, our hearts intertwine,
Lost in the moments where souls realign.

So let the fire burn for as long as it will,
In the hearth of our love, our spirits to thrill.
For even as embers begin to grow dim,
The flame's embrace holds each secret within.

Shades of Ruby Blues

The world paints a canvas, in crimson and hue,
Where passion's sweet whispers turn skies into blue.
A melody lingers in every bold stroke,
Breathless and vivid, like words that we spoke.

Ruby red sunsets, they spill through the trees,
Carrying dreams on the soft evening breeze.
Each shade tells a story of longing and loss,
The colors remind us of love's heavy cost.

In shades of the twilight, our secrets unfold,
A dance in the dazzle of stories retold.
Between every brush, a heartbeat is traced,
In the gallery of time, love's art is embraced.

So let us create in this twilight's embrace,
With strokes of affection, with gentle grace.
In patterns of ruby, the blues intertwine,
A masterpiece formed as our bodies align.

In silence, we linger where colors remain,
Echoes of laughter, the pulse of a pain.
Each shade is a promise of lifelong retreat,
In the gallery of the heart, where we meet.

The Seams of Infatuation

In the fabric of dreams, our threads start to pull,
Stitched tight like a secret, enchanting and full.
Whispers unspoken, they linger and dwell,
Each glance a needle, I know all too well.

Your smile is a stitch in the quilt of my heart,
A pattern emerging, a beautiful art.
The moments we gather, in time's gentle seam,
Each tapestry woven with whispers of dream.

In laces of longing and fabric of bright,
We chase through the day, surrender to night.
The seams pull us closer, no distance too vast,
Bound by the longing of echoes from past.

With needle and thread, let's create our own fate,
In a world where the beauty of love won't wait.
The seams of infatuation hold tight and true,
Binding our hearts in a dance just for two.

Through colors of passion, we find our own place,
In patterns entwined, there's no need for grace.
Though time may unravel the fabric we wear,
The seams of our hearts will remain ever rare.

Fiery Pathways

Beneath the vast skies, where dreams take flight,
We wander through shadows, chasing the light.
With every bold step, a spark in our gaze,
Navigating heartbeats through love's fiery maze.

The pathways unfurl in a dance of the brave,
Leading us forward, our souls they will save.
With flames at our heels, we journey together,
No storms can extinguish the bonds that we tether.

In echoes of laughter, the night becomes gold,
Each corner we turn, new stories unfold.
Through trials and triumphs, our spirits ignite,
On the fiery pathways, we chase the moonlight.

Let's traverse this journey, where hearts start to roam,
Finding the places that feel just like home.
In shadows and embers, we'll carve out our way,
Together forever, come night or come day.

The world is aflame with the choices we make,
In every shared moment, new sparks that awake.
For in fiery pathways, our spirits will soar,
Discovering love and so much more.

Woven in Crimson

In the twilight glow we weave,
Threads of stories, dreams to cleave.
Colors blend, a tapestry bright,
Woven in crimson, love takes flight.

Whispers soft through the night air,
Secrets shared with tender care.
Each stitch binds more than mere cloth,
A connection deeper than both.

Patterns shift like our emotions,
Rivers of trust, vast as oceans.
Under the moon, shadows caress,
Woven in crimson, pure tenderness.

The loom of fate turns and twirls,
Crafting bonds like delicate pearls.
Every thread tells of desire,
Woven in crimson, hearts aflire.

In this fabric, we find our way,
Guided by love's gentle sway.
Hand in hand, our hearts entwined,
Woven in crimson, forever aligned.

The Fabric of Desire

In every thread, a silent plea,
The fabric of desire, wild and free.
Stitched with hopes, a soft embrace,
Yearning whispers in this sacred space.

Colors dance, a passionate flame,
Patterns shifting, never the same.
In twilight's fabric, secrets spun,
The fabric of desire, two become one.

Each woven tale, a heart's confession,
Delicate passions, a bold expression.
With every knot, our dreams ignite,
The fabric of desire, pure delight.

Through dusk and dawn, our spirits soar,
In tangled threads, we seek for more.
Each moment cherished, time spent wise,
The fabric of desire never lies.

Together we mend, and together we fray,
In this woven world, love leads the way.
For in each layer our souls conspire,
The fabric of desire, our burning fire.

Hues of a Fiery Heart

Hues of a fiery heart unfold,
Crimson and gold like stories told.
Each brush stroke paints a moment true,
In a canvas bright, we find our hue.

Embers flicker in twilight's hold,
Passions ignited, brave and bold.
In a swirl of color, we dive deep,
Hues of a fiery heart, a love to keep.

With every shade, our souls converse,
In vibrant tones, the universe.
A dance of feelings, raw and free,
Hues of a fiery heart are we.

Through stormy nights and sunny days,
Our love shifts like the sun's warm rays.
In every glance, a spark's delight,
Hues of a fiery heart burn bright.

Together we craft our art divine,
In colors rich, our spirits shine.
Side by side, our dreams take flight,
Hues of a fiery heart, pure light.

The Dance of Burgundy

In a room alive with rhythm and grace,
The dance of burgundy finds its place.
Silks swirl softly, as visions twine,
Lost in the moment, your heart next to mine.

Each twirl whispers stories untold,
With every step, our spirits unfold.
This tapestry woven with laughter and cheer,
The dance of burgundy, drawing us near.

Eyes locked in a trance, swirling delight,
Under the stars, we embrace the night.
Footsteps echo, a melody sweet,
The dance of burgundy, our hearts skip a beat.

In the shadows, secrets gleam bright,
As we sway together, lost in the night.
With hands intertwined, our souls ignite,
The dance of burgundy, pure and right.

As dawn approaches, we cherish the spin,
Each movement a canvas that draws us in.
Together we share one final glance,
The dance of burgundy, a timeless romance.

Salmon Skies at Dusk

The horizon blushes soft and warm,
As day begins to lose its form.
Colors blend in a gentle dance,
Nature's love in a fleeting glance.

Salmon hues in the twilight fair,
Whisper secrets in the air.
Clouds float by in a soothing way,
Cradling dreams of the coming day.

Birds soar high in blissful flight,
Chasing echoes of fading light.
Each cresting wave tells a tale,
Of adventures that never pale.

Beneath the sky, hearts tune anew,
Finding hope in a painted view.
As stars prepare to take their place,
The dusk wraps all in its loving grace.

In this moment, time seems to pause,
While nature breathes with a gentle cause.
Salmon skies, a soothing balm,
In the evening, all is calm.

Woven in the Sunset

Threads of gold in the evening weave,
Patterns dance as shadows leave.
The sky wears a cloak so bright,
Spinning yarns of day and night.

Fingers of light stroke the land,
Caressing gently, as if planned.
Cloaks of color wrap the trees,
Whispering soft on a cool breeze.

Hues of amber, shades of rose,
A painter's touch that softly glows.
Nature's fabric, rich and vast,
A memory of the day just passed.

With each layer, stories unfold,
Of dreams and memories wrapped in gold.
The sunset sighs, a final call,
Inviting beauty to enthrall.

In this tapestry of light,
We find solace in the night.
Woven threads in a symphony,
Binding hearts in harmony.

The Chromatic Embrace

In the palette of dusk, colors blend,
Whispers of light that never end.
Violet shades kissed by the sun,
A chromatic dance that's just begun.

Crimson dreams float through the air,
Each hue a secret, a tender prayer.
Emerald greens in a soft embrace,
Nature's canvas, a sacred space.

As shadows stretch across the ground,
In vibrant hues, our hopes are found.
Glistening points of a starry night,
Painting stories with pure delight.

Every shade tells a tale anew,
A symphony played in every hue.
In twilight's grasp, we lose our fears,
Wrapped in color, embraced by cheers.

The world transforms in this interlace,
A magical moment, a warm embrace.
In chromatic splendor, we find our space,
Forever touched by this loving grace.

Passion's Fiber

Threads of fire in the morning light,
Passion weaves through day and night.
With every pulse, our hearts ignite,
Binding us in pure delight.

Fingers entwined, the world feels right,
In shadows shared, our spirits bright.
Together we dance, so wild and free,
Living echoes of what will be.

Whispers soft, a lover's tune,
Underneath the silver moon.
In every laugh, in every sigh,
We find the strength to always try.

Passion's fabric, woven tight,
A masterpiece in love's true light.
Every moment a cherished gift,
Nurtured dreams, our spirits lift.

Through trials faced, our bond will grow,
In woven hearts, our passions flow.
Crafting life with every thread,
Weaving futures, where love is spread.

An Ode to Fuchsia Blush

In petals bright, the fuchsia glows,
A dance of color that softly flows.
Whispers of spring on gentle breeze,
Embracing hearts with blooming ease.

With vibrant hue, the world ignites,
A canvas painted with pure delights.
Each sunrise brings a fresh debut,
In nature's galas, love rings true.

Upon the vines, life intertwines,
A tapestry of endless lines.
In gardens fair, the fuchsia stands,
A serenade from nature's hands.

In twilight's glow, the shadows play,
A lingering charm that holds its sway.
The blush of dusk, a soft embrace,
In every corner, finds its place.

Oh fuchsia dream, so warm and bright,
You lead the heart into the night.
A gentle kiss from blossom's touch,
We cherish you, dear fuchsia blush.

Heartstrings in Vermillion

Threads of crimson softly weave,
In every pulse, the heart believes.
A rhythm found in every beat,
Where love and passion gently meet.

In vermillion shades, a symphony,
A song that sings of you and me.
Each note a whisper, soft and clear,
In this embrace, we have no fear.

In laughter shared, our souls unite,
As dawn gives way to starry night.
With every glance, oh how they shine,
In vermillion hues, our hearts align.

Through storm and calm, we brave the tide,
With every tear, we choose our side.
The tapestry of love's sweet song,
In vermillion, we both belong.

Oh heartstrings tied in radiant red,
With every word that's left unsaid.
In the dance of life, we twirl and spin,
In the warmth of love, we both begin.

Crimson Connections

Beneath the sky of deepened hue,
Where sunsets blend in fiery view.
The bonds we form through time and space,
In crimson threads, we find our place.

With every step, a story spun,
In twilight's glow, the day is done.
The heart's soft echo, a guiding light,
In shared moments, we reach new height.

Through laughter shared and sorrows too,
Crimson connections bind me to you.
In roots so deep, our spirits soar,
Together we are forevermore.

As seasons change and years unfold,
In every whisper, the tales are told.
With every heartbeat, love's refrain,
In crimson roots, we grow again.

Oh sacred bond, in shadows cast,
In every moment, a spell is cast.
Through storms and calm, we stand as one,
In crimson connections, love's begun.

Weaving in Scarlet

In twilight's glow, our dreams ignite,
With scarlet threads, we weave the night.
Each moment shared, a tapestry,
In colors bright of you and me.

Through fields of roses, hand in hand,
We forge a path, a sacred land.
In every smile, a tale unfolds,
A treasure rare that never grows old.

In laughter's echo, our spirits rise,
As starlit wishes paint the skies.
In scarlet hues, we find our way,
Through hidden dreams and bright ballet.

With gentle hands, we stitch and sew,
In love's design, the passion grows.
Through heartbeats shared, our vision clear,
In scarlet threads, we hold so dear.

Oh sacred art, our lives entwined,
In every gesture, love defined.
Together weaving, our stories blend,
In scarlet dreams, we shall transcend.

The Passionate Loom

In the quiet of night, the loom does weave,
Threads of gold and silver, they dance and cleave.
Each pull and twist, stories intertwine,
Creating a fabric, both yours and mine.

The shuttle flies fast, your heartbeat's song,
Patterns emerge where we both belong.
Crimson and azure, colors collide,
In this tapestry, our dreams reside.

Beneath the soft touch, the fibers blend,
Each knot and seam, a message we send.
Love stitched in silence, a promise anew,
In the fabric of time, it's just me and you.

The loom sings softly, the rhythm of fate,
Woven in moments, oh, isn't it great?
As we pull together, our hearts align,
In this passionate work, our souls combine.

With every new thread, we face the unknown,
Strength in the fabric that we have grown.
Together through storms, together through light,
In the loom of our love, everything feels right.

A Fabric of Longing

In the depths of night, my heart does yearn,
A fabric of longing, with each twist I turn.
Woven with shadows, stitched with a sigh,
Every thread whispers, as time drifts by.

The loom stands steady, a sentinel true,
Crafting my dreams, every thought of you.
In colors of twilight, the memories thread,
Between each heartbeat, all that's been said.

Each weave tells a tale, both tender and bold,
Of promises made and stories retold.
A tapestry rich with the hopes we hold,
In the fabric of longing, love's warmth unfolds.

Amidst the fibers, your essence remains,
Lingering softly, in joy and in pains.
With every new pattern, our spirits entwine,
In this fabric of longing, forever divine.

As daylight arrives, the threads shimmer bright,
Reflecting our journey, love's endless light.
Though gathered from sorrow, its beauty can grow,
In this fabric we weave, my heart's gentle glow.

The Tint of Love's Embrace

In the glow of dawn, a hue soft and bright,
The tint of love's embrace steals away the night.
Colors collide, as the moments unfold,
In the tapestry woven, our story is told.

Brushes of dreams paint the canvas with care,
Each stroke a whisper, more than just air.
The vibrance of laughter, the depth of a sigh,
In the tint of our love, we learn how to fly.

With each gentle stroke, our hearts resonate,
Palette of passion, we patiently create.
In shades of affection, our spirits unite,
In the canvas of longing, everything feels right.

Textures of joy, and fibers of trust,
In the embrace of love, it's more than just lust.
Pouring our souls into colors of fate,
The tint of love's embrace, a bond we create.

As twilight descends, hues begin to blend,
In the warm light of love, every moment can mend.
Together we flourish, as life spins and sways,
In the tint of love's embrace, forever we stay.

Threads of Courage

In the fabric of life, threads stand tall,
Woven with courage, they answer the call.
Each strand holds a story, of battles we face,
Stitched with resolve, we carve out our space.

Through storms we have weathered, the fibers grow strong,
In the tapestry woven, we learn to belong.
Colors of valor, shades of belief,
With each woven layer, we banish the grief.

Threads of courage speak louder than words,
Binding us close, like the song of the birds.
In the heart of the fabric, our strength shines bright,
Together we rise, in the dark and the light.

Each knot tells a tale, of triumph and pain,
The rhythm persists, like a sweet soft refrain.
With every new twist, we challenge despair,
In the threads of courage, we show that we care.

As the loom hums softly, we dance hand in hand,
Crafting our futures, together we stand.
In a world full of chaos, our spirits endure,
In the threads of courage, we find our cure.

www.ingramcontent.com/pod-product-compliance
Ingram Content Group UK Ltd.
Pitfield, Milton Keynes, MK11 3LW, UK
UKHW031956131224
452403UK00010B/500